MY FIRST LOOK

AT COMMUNITIES

SOME FARMING TOWNS ARE IN AREAS WITH BIG HILLS

A Farming Town

VALERIE BODDEN

CREATIVE EDUCATION

Published by Creative Education

P.O. Box 227, Mankato, Minnesota 56002

Creative Education is an imprint of The Creative Company

Designed by Rita Marshall

Photographs by Getty Images (Iconica, LOOK, National Geographic, Photographer's

Choice, Reportage, Stone, Taxi)

Printed in the United States of America

Library of Congress Cataloging-in-Publication Data

Bodden, Valerie. A farming town / by Valerie Bodden.

p. cm. — (My first look at communities)

Includes index.

ISBN-13: 978-1-58341-513-9

1. Cities and towns—Juvenile literature. 2. Farms—Juvenile literature. 3. Agriculture—

Juvenile literature. 4. City and town life—Juvenile literature. I. Title.

HT 152.B65 2007   307.76—dc22   2006019354

First edition 9 8 7 6 5 4 3 2 1

A Farming Town

In the Country

A farming town is a town with lots of farms around it. Farming towns can be found in the **country**. There are farming towns all over the world.

Most farming towns are small. Not many people live in them. There are houses in a farming town. There are a few stores, too. You can find lots of barns and **silos** around farming towns.

ON MANY FARMS, BARNS ARE PAINTED RED

Most farming towns do not have many roads. There is not a lot of traffic. But farming towns are still busy. Grown-ups work on the farms near the town. Kids play outside. Animals walk around. Tractors plow the fields.

LIVING IN A FARMING TOWN

Most of the people in farming towns live in houses. Most of the houses have big yards. The houses are usually spread far apart.

Some farming towns have their own fire departments. Most of the firefighters are **volunteers**.

FIREFIGHTERS ARE ALWAYS READY TO HELP

Many of the people who live near farming towns have a farm. They work on the farm. They feed the animals. They milk the cows. They work in the fields.

Some people who live in a farming town work in stores. Others work in restaurants. Some sell tractors.

A cow can make 100 pounds
(45 kg) of milk a day. That's as
much as a sixth-grader weighs!

Some farming towns have a school. Other farming towns do not have a school. The kids in those towns have to ride a bus to a school in another town.

ANIMALS EVERYWHERE

There are animals everywhere in farming towns. Lots of animals live on farms. Cows live on farms. So do horses. Pigs and sheep live on some farms. Some farms have ducks or chickens, too.

There are all kinds of farms,

including pumpkin farms,

tree farms, and bee farms.

IN THE SPRING, CHICKS AND PIGLETS ARE BORN

Some of the animals in farming towns are pets. Many people in farming towns keep dogs and cats as pets. Others keep rabbits or even goats!

There are also lots of **wild** animals in farming towns. You can find squirrels and raccoons in many farming towns. Foxes live near some farming towns. So do deer. Many kinds of birds make their homes in farming towns, too.

DEER LIKE TO EAT THE PLANTS IN FIELDS

Fun in the Country

Farming towns are fun places. You can look at the animals on the farms near the town. You can help feed them. You can watch tractors work in the fields.

Farming towns are great places to take long walks. You can ride your bike through farming towns, too. Some farming towns have good spots for picnics. Some have a pond or river to swim in.

Many farming towns have railroad
tracks running through them.
Trains help carry farmers' **crops** to stores.

BRIGHT ORANGE PUMPKINS ARE PICKED IN THE FALL

At night, farming towns are usually quiet. People go in the house. They turn out the lights. Then the whole town is dark. People go to bed. They get ready for another day of fun on the farm!

FARMING IS LOTS OF WORK, BUT IT CAN BE FUN, TOO

Hands-on: Make a Farm

Barns and silos can be found around farming towns. You can make a barn and silo for your own farm!

What You Need

A small cardboard milk carton

An empty toilet paper roll

Red and black tempera paints

Green construction paper

Paintbrushes

Glue

Markers

What You Do

1. Paint the milk carton red to look like a barn.
2. When the red paint is dry, use black paint to make doors for your barn.
3. Paint the toilet paper tube red to make a silo.
4. Glue the barn and silo on the construction paper.
5. Draw some animals on your farm!

FARMERS STORE HAY IN BARNS AND SILOS

Index

Words to Know

country—an area with lots of land but not many houses or other buildings

crops—plants that farmers grow in their fields

silos—tall, round buildings used to hold grain or animal food

volunteers—people who do things because they want to help out; they do not get paid

wild—an animal that is not a pet

Read More

Adamson, Heather. *A Day in the Life of a Farmer*. Mankato, Minn.: Capstone Press, 2004.

Gillis, Jennifer Blizin. *Farm Life*. Minneapolis: Compass Point Books, 2005.

Roop, Peter, and Connie Roop. *A Farming Town*. Des Plaines, Ill.: Heinemann Library, 1998.

Explore the Web

Elmo's Silly Mixed-up Farm http://www.sesameworkshop.org/sesamestreet/games/flash.php?contentId=10784400&

Farm Animals around the World http://www.enchantedlearning.com/coloring/farm.shtml

Welcome to the Farm http://www.msichicago.org/exhibit/farm